Genealogy Research
and
Those Photographs

*How to Keep Details of the People and Day
with Any Photo in a Permanent Way without
Altering the Original Photograph*

Genealogy Research and Those Photographs
How to Keep Details of the People and Day with Any Photo
in a Permanent Way without Altering the Original
Photograph
Copyright © 2015 D. KALTEN

iv

Contents

Introduction vii

Chapter One. Where You Start 1

Chapter Two. Step One 5

Chapter Three. Scan to Where 9

Chapter Four. Your Notes 13

Chapter Five. Saving Information 17

Chapter Six. The Trick 21

Chapter Seven. When 33

Chapter Eight. Adding Information 37

Chapter Nine. Printing Choices 41

Chapter Ten. Added Examples 43

Chapter Eleven. Main Steps in Summary 75

FREE programs 77

A note from the author. 79

vi

Introduction

Have you ever found old family photographs, looked at them and felt totally lost concerning who the people are that are shown in them? Maybe you have an inherited old family album with no notes, no names, no dates, nothing to even begin to give you a hint of what you are holding in your hands. You don't know who the people are, the year or years or where they were taken at. One or some of the photos may appear to be a special days but you have no idea what the events were.

As you begin to unravel the mysteries you hold, also think about the photographs that your parents and you have and will take, and begin documenting in a permanent way so information is not lost or lost again.

This book will show you how to document photographs and allow you to keep information with the photographs, but yet not alter the originals. Preservation and no damage are key factors.

Some avenues to finding answers with older photographs are:

(1) It is a profession photograph and shows the name and address of the photographer. You can determine the approximate year of the photograph by finding records of when that photographer was in business at that address.

(2) By comparing the style of clothing you are able to identify a time period.

(3) You can identify or recognize younger people in a group photograph which helps date the photograph. It also helps

by knowing the names of who that person would be related to.

(4) You find other family members who have the same or a similar photograph and they do have information about the person, place and maybe the year of the photograph.

(5) The process of elimination by face features where other photographs lead to that person being the same person as shown in other photographs but at another age. These would be categorized as 'Appears to be ...' along with your reasons for saying so.

This book does include photograph samples to guide and also give you ideas.

Chapter One. Where You Start

There you sit with a group of old photographs and you have absolutely no idea what you have. You don't know if it is from your mothers' family, your fathers' family or how many generations back they go. You wonder why someone in the past didn't at least put a name with the person or people shown in the views.

You don't know where to begin but you know you want to figure it out and you want to document it. You have figured out that you should scan it so you can email it to various family connections with hopes that you can get some answers. That scan is actually your first step with permanent documentation for that or those photos. This book will show you how to do it a little differently so you can clearly document and re-document if needed.

Following are some things you do want to know as they each help tell 'the story' concerning a photograph. You can actually put those questions as part of a view, but not on the photo being scanned, to email and later update your main 'working' view. This sounds a little confusing, but it will be explained a little further in this book.

You want to know:

(1) The name.

(2) The birth and death dates.

(3) Date or approximate date or year of the photo.

(4) Where was the photo taken at?

(5) Who took the photo?

(6) Was this a special day or event?

(7) Is there any special little story that should be attached to this photograph?

(8) You also do want to document who you are, where you got those photos from, and/or who gave them to you.

Be careful when you put a date. Do specify what that date is for such as a birth, death or photo date as one can always be thought to be one of the others. DOB is birth. DOD is death. Photo date is the date or approximate date of the photo. An approximation can be written as 'ca' and the year or year range.

Items you are not sure of or want further proof for, you can make the lettering red if you want to. Down the road, you will do your final 'work' with all the unknowns.

As you slowly manage to actually answer questions about an old photograph, you are documenting for your future family generations.

Have you thought of using a program that organizes information for photographs or organizes the photos alone? What would happen if that program no longer works with the changes that are sure to happen with the way computers read information and operate as years go by?

These pages will tell you how to add various details to a photograph, but not actually on the photograph so they won't get lost or deleted from the photo. You will also find out how you can print those details, if you want to, as part of a digital scan (part of the newly formed photograph) or separately if you would like to. You will be able to print out 'the details' only, if wanted, to keep a copy with your actual original photograph.

An example of details, as you may choose, with documentation can actually read as follows.

John Robert SMITH
Son to Gabriel SMITH & Martha Mae JONES
DOB ca 1798 VA – DOD June 3, 1881 Richmond, VA
Photo date: ca 1861 - 1865 Civil War Uniform
Photo place: Unknown
Photo handed down to son, John Robert JR; to his son, Samuel A.; to his son, Samuel A. JR; to his daughter in 2015, Mary Margaret (SMITH) GRIMES.
You can also add a condensed blurb concerning his military history and other important detail here.

.

4

Chapter Two. Step One

Having a large interest in genealogy, I was always writing dates, names and a short little photo summary on the back of currently taken photo snapshots and professionally taken current photographs. Meanwhile, I was always on the lookout for old photographs that family members may have had. When I was lucky to come across some old treasures while chasing unmet distant family members, there was very rarely any type of information on the back of the photographs. To make matters worse, the person who owned the photograph usually did not have any idea who the person was. I would borrow the photograph to scan the front and back of those photographs so the owner could quickly get their original back. My hopes were always there to find more photographs somewhere and somehow that matched to that person and that it or they would lead to some answers.

I would hand write all the information given to me by the photograph owner on my big paper notepad such as whose photograph album it came from or who owned the box of photographs that it was found in. When back home I would measure the original and write those measurements down. If there was a photography studio name on it, I would track that business down through old city directories or through city historical areas. This gave me a city for the person in the photo. Sometimes a photographer would add their address on the photograph and maybe was in business at that address for only a few years before they moved elsewhere or went out of business. I would document the years that the photographer was operational at that address as that gave me a time frame. Of course clothing, the type of photograph and the possible items in the back ground also helps date a photograph.

With the photograph scans I had to decide how I wanted to file them in my computer. More on this is in my book titled *'Genealogy Research: How to Organize the Notes, Papers, Documents, Emails, Scans, Computer Files, and Photographs for Family Research'*.

Once I was organized, I was very busy with scanning as is described in this book that you are now reading.

...

To start, sort the photographs before you go any further. If you have a lot of them, inexpensive, letter size, white envelopes can help sort and you can make notes on the envelopes. Use a mechanical pencil as wet ink can easily be accidentally smeared over to photographs.

Do not write on any envelope if you have photographs in it. Remove the photo/s, write, and then reinsert the photographs.

As you sort, you may find that two or more of the photographs were actually taken on the same day per the people, the clothing &/or the background shown. By having the photographs pre-grouped, this will save you a lot of aggravation later with adding information and eliminate searches for what you have already found. It also eliminates going back through things done and having to redo them.

An example of grouping similar photos: Say you have seven photographs all taken on a boat and everyone is wearing the same clothing. Put all seven into one envelope.

If at all possible, try to set the envelopes in a time frame with the oldest on top. With pencil, put the year of the photograph, if known, in the upper right corner of the envelope. If you are guessing on a year, put 'ca' and the year in the upper right corner of the envelope so that it reads (example) ca 1930.

...

A tip on using the envelopes: If you are working with photographs that you have borrowed from a family member, you can actually take envelopes with you when you get the photos if the person is willing to spend time with you to furnish any information they know. You can write notes on the envelopes and insert the photo/s after writing. Always have a pad of paper ready too as you can do your paper notes per photo and insert that into each envelope. Sometimes an envelope does not give enough room to write down all the information furnished so have a pad of paper ready.

...

Sometimes the owner of photographs thinks they can tell you everything they know in five minutes concerning the photographs they have, but it is soon apparent they know much more about the family. Usually the talk can get around to various types of family information. If agreeable to all parties, take at least a tape recorder to use as a backup for information as at times the pencil just doesn't want to write as fast as the words are spoken.

...

If you think you can get through a lot of photographs with documentations in a short amount of time, and you do plan on doing your project as accurately as possible, don't rush yourself. It is a lot faster to think things out before you do something rather than have to go back and redo things.

You will find some photographs are easy and others may take years for one little fact to drop into your lap. That is where you must have an organized system with your photo organization project.

*

Chapter Three. Scan to Where

You should now have all the photographs sorted and your notes organized. The next step is getting your computer ready for the notes and scans of the photographs.

Before you start scanning, you need to have a place to file them. The fact is that you do need to have a place for placement of those scans you will scan.

The following noted folders can be in any place you choose to store them within your computer. You may want to at least start a folder that is named 'Photographs Unknown' -OR- 'Unknown Photographs' on your main screen and place all photographs and notes for the photographs in there for now. Remember your computer can do searches and the first word you use is important.

For photographs from one person (not of one person) make a subfolder showing who you got the photo/s from. As an example, say you got the photos from Joe Jones, make a folder saying 'Unknown Photos from Joe Jones'. There can be any amount of folders within that folder, those inserted folders being sub-folders.

The actual photograph scans and your notes (your Word Document notes - more on this follows) will be in those sub-folders. IF you only had one photograph FROM a person, you could do just one folder with no sub-folder. I'll explain this in two examples. You substitute the name which is used here for clarification.

One photograph only furnished from a person: Name the folder 'Photo Unknown from Joe Jones'. This is a subfolder to 'Photos Unknown'.

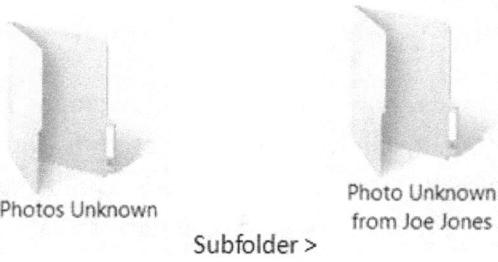

Photos Unknown

Subfolder >

Photo Unknown
from Joe Jones

If you have more than one photograph furnished from a person: Make a folder saying 'Photos Unknown from Joe Jones'. This is a subfolder to 'Photos Unknown'.

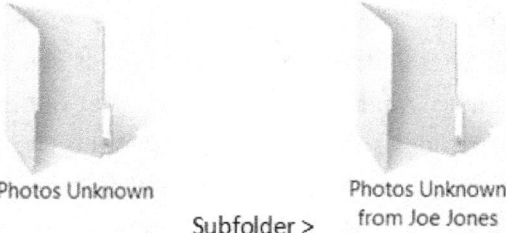

Photos Unknown

Subfolder >

Photos Unknown
from Joe Jones

Within the 'Photos Unknown from Joe Jones' folder you will make subfolders. Open the folder and make new folders within that folder (level 3 of folders) naming the folders as 'Photo Unk 01 from Joe Jones', 'Photo Unk 02 from Joe Jones', and so on. Each subfolder will house the scans and the notes for each single photograph. You can add any short additional words to the end of your labels if wanted. An example: Woman w bun. Keep wording short.

A visual of your folders for level 3 will be:
Photos Unknown >
Photos Unk from Joe Jones >
and further subfolders showing the photo number you gave it.

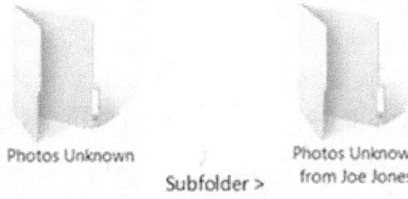

Photos Unknown

Subfolder >

Photos Unknown from Joe Jones

Subfolders within 'Photos Unknown from Joe Jones'

Photo UNK 01 from Joe Jones

Photo UNK 02 from Joe Jones

Photo UNK 03 from Joe Jones woman w bun

If you have a few photos that were taken on the same day, use your own judgement if you want to possibly do each for a separate folder or do all into one folder. You may choose to do them into one folder (such as 'Photos UNK 01 from Joe Jones') and then do subfolders within it. The advantage with all into one folder if taken on the same day is that any information found should match in some way to all of them for that day.

...

When naming and numbering folders, it may help if you do keep a paper and pencil by you for keeping track of what you are doing. Any interruption can easily lead to you forgetting what step you are working on for the photograph folders.

...

If you DO know who the person is in a photo, you will not save it to an Unknown photo folder. You want to file it in a person's folder. You can keep building information concerning the photo in a Word Document as you will for the unknown photographs, adding the information to the photo when you are ready to do so. Remember that you do want to keep the photo and its notes (your word document notes) in one subfolder named as such for that person or people in the photograph/s.

When complete, you can do a copy and paste to each 'MAIN person folder' as explained in *'Genealogy Research: How to Organize the Notes, Papers, Documents, Emails, Scans, Computer Files, and Photographs for Family Research'*.

*

Chapter Four. Your Notes

Previously mentioned is doing a Word Document for each photograph to hold your notes for that photograph. If you do not have the Microsoft Word Document program you can download a FREE word program:

http://www.openoffice.org/download/index.html

...

A computer word program will allow you to get organized without a lot of 'flying' paper notes. As you may need to change information or add to your notes, it is easy to do. Just be sure to do a SAVE after any changes. This is NOT your final work. It is a way to get organized with your information and also allows you to see how you may want your information to show as you later organize the information to add to a photograph. That Word Document is added to the same folder that holds the photograph scan.

Naming your Word Document would be the same as your file folder name. You can even add a copy of the photo but size it down after INSERTING (not copy & paste) it to the Word Document.

An example of things to keep track of in your Word Document, and it can vary wildly with each, is:

(1) The name of the person in the photograph.
(2) The date or approximate year or time frame of the photo.
(3) The birth and death dates.
(4) The place of birth and death.

(5) The name of the parents.

(6) The names of the children the person had.

(7) The name of who owns the original photograph and how they are connected to you.

(8) The name of the person who scanned the photo and the scan date.

(9) The size of the original photograph and any notes about it.

(10) Where, when and how the owner got the photograph.

(11) Any family story told about the original owner &/or how the photo was passed down through the family.

(12) The thoughts of the current photograph owner concerning the photograph.

(13) Any other details discovered such as the previously noted photographer and their business history or any possible special note such as the location that the photograph was taken at.

One example of a special note, which is extensive details in this example, concerns a very early photograph I found in a used book store. The photograph was of a man and was glued into the back of an 1868 published book. The book was published in limited quantity and the subject was a person who fought in the American Revolution, dying in 1814.

The photograph was thick and had lettering indented into the front that said 'COPY'. Per the subject of the book being an ancient family member I knew that photograph had to fit into the family somehow. There was also a hand written note in the front of the book that gave the previous owners name, a woman, and further hand written was 'Life of Great Grandfather'. I spent many hours tracking the children of the American Revolution veteran and the photograph turned out to be a grandson to one of the brothers to one of my 5th great-grandmothers. I further learned that he was also a somewhat well-known author. The woman who wrote her name and the note in the book was the daughter to the man in the photograph. There was a lot of detail that needed to be kept with that photograph as I couldn't imagine anyone else spending the multi-hours I did with tracking the facts. The person was not a direct tie to me but working in genealogy, I had a face to match to a family name, a notable name in the historic archives of books.

Following is the hand written note in the front of the book.

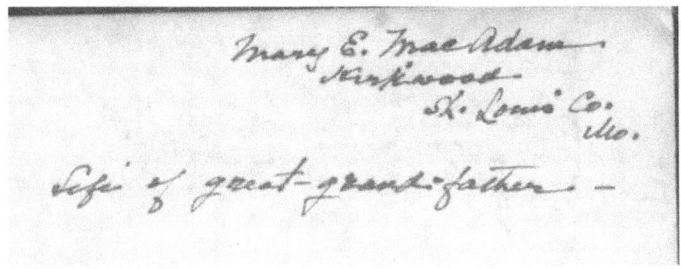

The next view is the old, thick photograph that was glued into the book. It is shown as it was glued crooked onto the black inside covering. It is a light photo and the eyes are now actually holes where the cardboard stock has been eaten through over the years by chemicals from the photograph. I do have various sizes and alterations saved in JPEG format. No added information by me is shown in this view.

...

The end result that you are working for at this point should be for the contents of the yellow computer folder which holds (1) a scan of the photo front, (2) a scan of the photo back and (3) the Word Document summary typed from the notes for what you know and had done so far concerning finding information for that photograph. More on these things follow.

Now you know what to do with all of those unknowns. As you work through the following pages, file your results in those folders.

Be sure to do backups in case of computer problems.

Chapter Five. Saving Information

Your options

Let's say you now have a name for a person or for the people in a photograph. What are your options for keeping the information with the newly formed photo (your scan) after you have scanned it? There are five.

1. You can add information into the Comments area. That is found with a right click on the scanned photograph under Properties, Details and then Comments for the photograph.

There are two main problems with this. First if someone or some strange program clears out the metadata, the information is lost. Secondly, if you print the photo, the information does not print and there is no neat format for it under the Comments area. This area would at least be good to name the person who owns the photograph if you do not know a name for the subject. You could also add the name of the person in the photo, the current owner and date scanned along with by whom. You may want to add your name as the scan person along with the date only. I myself leave the comments area blank as I have placed it WITH the photo.

2. You can insert the photo into a Word Document, type out your information and save it as a Word Doc or a PDF.

That is fine if you are quickly getting a copy of your work to someone but would you consider that an archival item? Are you sure you want this as your final work to pass down to the family members? What if you want a true JPG or TIFF copy with the information?

3.   You can insert your photograph view into a Word Document, type out your information and then do a screen shot, saving that as a JPEG/JPG.

Again, would you consider that an archival item? What if you want a true JPEG or TIFF copy that can be printed per size choice and with the information?

4. You can try to keep a Word Document with each photo for eternity.

Do you really think the two would stay together through the ages between computer changes and the way different people think, as if you think everyone will understand that there is information there? It also requires two printings.

5. This #5 is what this book is about.

You will have a true duplicate of the photograph with the choice to print it out in the size you want, with and without the information attached to the photograph. The words can be part of the photo or printed separately and added to the back of a newly printed photograph. This works well if you are using a clear see through frame or a double frame.

...

At this point, there is one thing to add concerning any hand written notes you may have taken while talking to another person or other people about the photos.

You can scan your notes to your main folder titled 'Photos Unknown' and place them in the folder for whom you received the photographs from. This is a good idea so that you do have an original copy in case of any future questions or confusions that may come up. It would be best to scan those notes as a PDF, assuming you have more than one page. If you are unfamiliar with how to scan for a PDF: Scan > Save As > PDF. Use the dropdown arrow that your scanner should have to choose the PDF option. Don't forget to scan notes on envelopes too.

Label your scanned notes (example) 'Original Notes from Joe Jones' (using the name that applies). If you did a voice tape recording or video tape, you can add a copy to that file folder also.

*

Chapter Six. The Trick

With your photographs organized in envelopes, your computer files started and your notes organized into a word document program and into the folder named for the photograph, you are now going to actually scan your photographs and place them into the folders named for them.

You should have at least one folder ready and named with the 01 in the heading. If you are dealing with over 99 photographs FROM one person, name them with three digits, your first being with 001. If you have over 999 photographs from one person, name them with four digits, your first being 0001. An example of a first label for a group of photographs from one person who has furnished over 1000 photographs, rare but it happens, is: 'Photo UNK 0001 from Joe Jones'.

Should you know who the person is in the photograph you will NOT name the photo as unknown and you will NOT file the photo in a Photo Unknown folder. You will save it to a person's folder, that being a folder with the persons name on it. You will label your known photo as (examples) '1921 JONES Mary PHOTO', 'JONES Mary 1921 Photo', 'Photo 1921 JONES Mary'. Think out what format you want to use and use it for all known photos for everyone. Remember your choice of the format also such as JPEG, TIFF or both.

When scanning for placement into a person's folder, you can make a photo file for it on your main screen, then drag that folder to the persons file folder when you are done with that photo. It's easier with your 'saves'.

...

For scanning I strongly suggest you first practice with a current nothing snapshot so that you do get a small amount of practice and understand the goal of what you are going to do. This will help eliminate any fading from the older ones that you really want to take care with.

When scanning, make a rule for yourself on the formats you want to use. For black and white photos, do you want to scan in black and white and also in color? If I have aging photos that are yellowed (sepia tone) I do both versions.

Rule #1: Scan the back first. If the back has any information on it, scan it. Get the back out of the way. I always scan the back, even if it appears blank, as it is later proof that there was nothing on the back.

There was a time when scanning what I thought was a blank back brought out very light lettering that was not noticed. Through darkening, it was readable. Saving the back as a JPEG is usually OK unless you want a higher quality for it. Save this as (example) 'Photo UNK 01 back from Joe Jones'.

Rule #2: NOTE: You are going to do a little something extra when you do your scan of the front.

Put the photograph on the scanner. Do NOT put it tight against the edge or touching the top area of the scanner. You want to leave a little bit of space between the scanner edge and the photograph edges. It can be a wide area if that works best for you. You do want to get the photograph perfectly straight on the scanner so this may take a little patience. Sometimes it helps to set something that is thin, flat and heavy on the photograph to keep it from moving.

Taping a few quarters side by side on to a small piece of cardboard will work. Make sure the cardboard is NOT as wide or long as the photograph. SLOWLY close your scanner lid to scan because you do not want the photograph to move. This closed lid will give you a white background.

If the photograph is not straight, correct it and rescan. You choose your resolution with your scans. I prefer a higher quality than my scanner tends to pick for me.

Rule #3: You are going to scan BUT you are going to over scan past the outside edges of the photograph. I actually over scan past the edges on the back sides also. If you look at the scan from that book I previously mentioned, you will see the ENTIRE photograph. This was glued on black paper so it is easy to see those photograph edges.

Rule #4: IMPORTANT! After the scan is run but before you save the view, you are going to crop OUTSIDE of the photograph. Not at or on the photograph. You are going to crop to allow a small amount of extra space at the top, the two sides and you are going to PULL a large BLANK space into the bottom below the photograph. Try to guess how much space you will need to add all of your information below the photo in a condensed, sensible manner. If you allow more space than needed that is OK and better for now. You will crop to a perfect size later after information is added. Scan at 100% size which makes it a true replica of the original photograph.

You may choose to save your view as a TIFF and ALSO as a JPEG at this time, putting both in the folder you have made for this photograph. As it saves to your computer it will show the type of format at the end of the heading. You do not need to scan a second time to save twice unless your scanner demands it.

At this time you may choose to do a scan x 300% &/or 500% too. Just label each as such. An example on noting size: REYNOLDS Mary 1921 photo bwx500%.jpg. The 'bw' would mean black and white.

Following shows you your 'blank' scan. Later information was added and saved with another name so that I always have my 'blank' in case any changes need to be done or information added. NOTE. It is wise to save a blank rewording it prior to adding words. Example: REYNOLDS Mary 1921 photo words bwx500%.jpg

Remember, naming is your filing system so you may choose to start a heading with the year and not the name.

In the following first view, I have given the entire cropped area shading so that you can see the full area being saved for text for this photograph. Without the shading the white blank area would not show on a white book page. Next to it is the finished version. A small amount of information was added to the photo bottom edge in case printing was wanted for only the photo. In retrospect, I would rather have all that wording below the photo. The last row of wording tells who scanned the photo along with the year and month that the scan was done. I will be redoing this one as I save all my blanks. That means I do not need to rescan the photo to change the words. A new save with a new label was done once the text was added.

1952 Dec
Our FIRST sister photo!

Donna (the oldest), Gail (holding the baby),
and Carey (the baby).
Living room, tree in outside front corner.
11093 Nashville, Detroit 05, Mich. (as it was wrote then).

Carey now has the chair.
Our mom had trim on the chair that is the drapery
material. I'm fairly sure she made the drapes
as also the couch cover, ect.

I remember when this was taken.
I had a fit because I could not hold the baby.
Our parents said 'help hold' which really didn't 'fly'.

Photo scanned by Donna M. ST. FELIX 2009 July

QUESTION: While you have the photograph in the perfect place for scanning, do you also want to do an enlargement as previously mentioned, or maybe an enlargement crop into any special area? Slowly look over the photograph for what could be interesting. Four examples for why I ask this:

(1) My maternal grandmothers' brother-in-law used to work on a boat in Holland. I had a very small, old yellowed photograph taken around 1910 that I played around with concerning size and crops. What I thought was an old rag on his pants turned out to be a giant hole in his pants and the strange shoes he had on were muddy wooden shoes. The boat was full of potatoes where originally I couldn't tell what was in that boat but it looked like blankets or some type of material.

(2) The father to my paternal grandfather used to make his own home made elixir of sorts, something I thought that people drank. The photograph I had was taken, so I figured out, about 1909. He was on a podium in front of a tent that had an emblem on the entrance that looked like an oval but no detail could be seen. I enlarged and sharpened it to the point where I could see it was the image of a bathtub. I realized then that his elixir was for bathing. It was apparent that at various places &/or events he would set up his tub and tent and invite people to take a bath. I never did figure out if he definitely had hot water but I think he did. Through the enlargements I was able to identify his oldest son and small granddaughter, the son being a large strong man, strong enough to carry water from a fire pit (the days when life was so different). He had his shirt sleeves rolled up so he was apparently working although in the view he was walking as he waved at the camera. The photo was a professional one which I assume he traded some of his goods for the photo.

(3) In a photograph of a great-great grandmother, it appeared there was a flaw in the photo on her hair area where two white spots stood out. Thanks to enlargements it shows that it was a piece of hair jewelry. The white spots look like a pearl on each end of what looks like a type of stick pin.

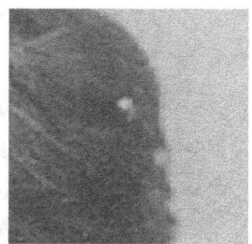

(4) A cousin has a rather large, professionally taken group photo taken in 1935 that is at eighteen inches wide by over a foot high. I had to have an office supply store scan the full photo and I got that on disk from them. I also scanned it on one of their printers that printed large paper with the results being an excellent quality. However, on my scanner I was able to do a few enlarged scans of the original to get everyone into my views. With those enlarged scans I was able to do a decent photograph from crops of everyone. The main photograph and four random views of many from it follow.

The 1935 main family group photograph.

Above: One crop. The oldest couple (front row left).

Above: Crop. Middle row, left standing.

Above: Crop. Child, front sitting.

Above. Crop. A husband, wife and daughter from the middle area of the photograph

Most of the people in the previous group photograph were identified. Some of the crops are still sitting in an UNK folder.

...

NOTE: If you are working with crops as shown from the group photograph, you will have to (1) save your scan (example: JONES Bob 1935 crop original.jpg).

(2) Then insert that scan of a person into a Word Document.

(3) Crop that Word Document leaving blank space below the photo, that space being to later add words. Free programs such as MWSnap are easy to use for this. Save it to the same folder with changing the label a little. Something to reflect that it is a blank is best. (example: JONES Bob 1935 crop blank space.jpg)

(4) When you are ready to add words, copy that last save and do another save naming it to reflect wording is in it. Add your wordings and do a screen shot (using a program such as MWSnap), saving it as a JPG/JPEG/TIFF. Adding wording can be done with most photo programs such as the FREE FastStone Image Viewer.

...

After you do your scans, using your program of choice, remove all Metadata. In the program FastStone Image Viewer you click on Tools > Remove JPEG Metadata > Remove All. This makes the size of your view less 'meaty'. You can add information into the comments area if you want, after that removal.

...

Before moving forward and adding words to your photograph, test both your TIFF and JPEG that were saved, assuming you have saved both. Is your computer able to open the TIFF view? If not, you just need a computer with more ability. As far as putting your words onto a view, you will then choose to put your words with your JPG/JPEG views. In the future you can copy them from your Word Document onto your TIFF view.

...

You have your scans done and now you are ready to add information to whatever view you think you have all the information for.

*

Chapter Seven. When

Concerning putting the information you have WITH the photograph, you will only do this once and only when you KNOW who the person is, unless you reach a point that you do not want to pursue that photograph any further. You can add whatever you have for the photograph but if you find a name, you will be redoing your work or you will have to do a patch in, if you leave space to do so. It has been my experience that when you find a name, you usually find more information so just wait to add anything directly. Just keep your Word Document updated.

Once you have completed your work with the photograph, that meaning having added the information to the large blank area of the scan of the photograph, you will rename the folder for the person IN the photograph and file it elsewhere. See my published organization book noted previously titled '*Genealogy Research: How to Organize the Notes, Papers, Documents, Emails, Scans, Computer Files, and Photographs for Family Research*'.

If there is more than one known person shown, you can copy and paste a copy to each person.

...

34

Following is an example of an add-in onto the photo description. The add-in is under the right side of the photograph and tells who wrote the year 1922 on the photo. This is also an example of a badly done description. The wording is too large, there should be no add-in, the person who did the scan is not named, the date of the scan is not shown, and the owner and history of the photo is not shown. The original is blurry but it's about all that exists for the woman. The back is also shown. Both of these were scanned in color which shows in sepia tone although they show in black and white in this book.

1922 Detroit, Michigan   *Date wrote by Tillie or Jake FLINT,*
their oldest brother.
Geezina (ZWEEP) FLINT [Dutch Immigrant] and daughters
- American names -
Marie Elizabeth [later for a while RALEY] & Anne Christine [later ST. FELIX].

Per Marie: This was torn down for a highway.

Chapter Eight. Adding Information

To add the information to the photograph you will be using a separate program and there are many FREE ones out there that can do this. They operate basically the same but I will be referring to the free program FastStone Image Viewer from www.FastStone.org. I have no connection to that viewer or company other than I find it easy to use.

...

After downloading the program:

1. Right click on the photo you want to work on. You want to choose what program to open the view with. You want FastStone Viewer (or whatever you choose to work with).

You may have to click or double click on your screen a few times if a large black screen shows your photo. It depends on your program and various versions of programs.

2. You should see a blue line around the photo you will be working on. Look above and you should see what looks like a yellow box with excess in the lines shown on an icon. That is the crop tool. Left click on it.

3. With your mouse you will see a plus sign. Move it to 'crop' an area that you want to save. In this case, you want to make the space on the top, the right and left sides of your scan even. You do want to leave a little bit of space between the outer photo edge and your crop as you do want the entire full photograph, including the edges, to show. Do NOT crop away at any space at the bottom area of your photograph at this time.

4. Click on the word Crop. Save it giving it a NEW name. That can be as simple as adding crop to front of the description. Do not delete any description that is there. It should automatically save to the same folder which now will give you two views after this save.

5. Assuming you have your word document notes all wrote out and streamlined, all being ready as you want things to read, you can possibly either copy and paste the words into the blank space or type it out. You want to do this into the second view you just cropped. It depends on your computer and its ability for which way will work for you. Leave the first scan alone as it is your original for reuse if needed.

To add the words click on your just saved crop:

a. Click on the ABC icon.

b. Click on the A on the far left.

c. A box will open. Drag the top of the box to where you want to start your first line, drag the sides almost to the sides, and drag the bottom all the way to the bottom.

d. Begin typing (if you cannot paste into it). Usually the black text is what you want. You may be able to 'Bold' it also.

e. Adjust the size of the text using the Text Style box that opens. Usually the top line is the largest (size 12 or 14) with the lowest line being a size 8, the smallest. You can highlight any line to change the size.

f. When everything is entered, drag the text box to center it below your photo close to the photo. Your goal is to balance (center) the text under the photograph.

g. Save your view giving it a 3rd name. Open it to make sure the text you typed in is as you want it. If not, your original and your first crop are still there to start over.

h. When the text is as you want it, it is now time to crop out any excess space under the text. Do leave a small amount of blank space. Resave it with a fourth name. This is your finished product.

i. That's it. You are done with that photo. You may want to change the name (the label) for your photo. You DO want to keep your original scan, your first cropped scan, the back of the photo scan, your word document summary and your finished product as you never know what may need to be added or later adjusted. An example for a new folder name is: '1939 Photo JONES, Mary 1870-1942', the last set of numbers being the birth and death years. Drag the photo folder to the older for the person.

If you want to test a printing, use cheap paper to see how the layout is. If you want to keep a printing, use good quality photo paper. More on printing follows.

Chapter Nine. Printing Choices

Printing choices for size will depend upon the original photo, the amount of information added, the purpose for the photo and the size wanted. Keep in mind that for some sizes printed, you will need to do matting within a frame as the wording throws normal sizes off.

To print only the photo, in the original size with no added wording showing: Crop to it and print. You can save that with a new label such as '1939 Mary JONES photo only'.

To print only the words, crop to the words and print. You can resave that with a new label such as '1939 Mary JONES words only'.

With both of the new saves, you can size those to what you want when printing if you want larger or smaller than the original. A reminder: An original size is scanned x 100%. It is an excellent idea to list the size with the label. An example for this, done in black & white is: TAYLOR Jim 1912 Photo bw x100%. For color change the bw to what works for you. I use 'col' in place of the bw.

...

Remember when you are changing sizes of an original for printing only and then you decide you want to save it, do not save it without changing the label. If you do not change the label, you will change the size of the original. It is a good idea to open a view and save it with a new label (say adding 5x7) then alter that new save, resave and print.

...

To actually keep the information with the original photos that should be protected and put away, you can print out your best new photo with the information, insert it into an archival vinyl folder and put it at the bottom of the box with the original. The vinyl folders come with holes for notebooks if you choose to use those. Do NOT set the originals into those folders with the printout. use a separate folder.

*

Chapter Ten. Added Examples

Examples are shown here to give you ideas for what you can do and tips are shown among them.

Each view under each example is a photo in itself. That does include a view with more than one view shown as it is now all one photo in the new save that was done. Any part can be cropped to in order to print a section of choice from the photo but as noted in this book, you should have those separate photos saved. That crop, as with any view shown here, can be resized prior to printing to print without a resave of it.

Each view shows writing that has been added to the newly formed JPEG (photo). The writing was not added to the book text.

Each view that contains more than one view has all views saved separately. They were copied and combined to make one view with multi-views so all views show at once. This means if you are viewing a page that has three or four views in it, each view is saved as a separate JPEG (photo) and the combined view is a new save. The folder they are kept in will contain four or more JEPG's for the photograph. This will make more sense as you see the examples.

Each view can be printed from the JPEG at the size of choice. Changing nothing with sizing for printing the view will print at the size I saved it at. All views were scanned at 100% (full size) and many had enlargements also done.

In summary, this gives a wide choice for sharing with others with the group views in one JPEG (photo) being the easiest.

References to a color photograph will show in black & white in this book.

Names have been removed from most views for this book.

Following are the examples.

Example #1

In this example which shows four views, the back was scanned at 100% and also x 300%. The enlargement (x 300%) was cropped for a second save and is shown here.

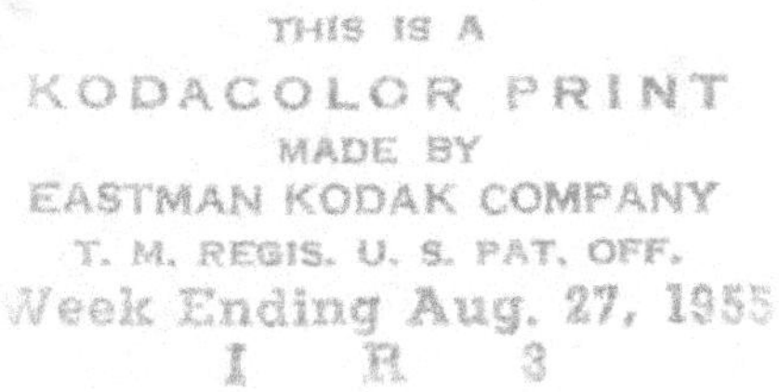

THIS IS A
KODACOLOR PRINT
MADE BY
EASTMAN KODAK COMPANY
T. M. REGIS. U. S. PAT. OFF.
Week Ending Aug. 27, 1955
I R 3

The following view shows the original photo, the 'Kodacolor' of the time frame, has faded over time. The original that was scanned had a lot of wording added and shows all the names but they were cropped out for this book entry. Note that the description with it is part of the newly formed photograph. It was not added for book text. Above is from the back.

A second view is shown with a black boarder. That was generated with a free on line program. That appears to mute the colors further.

Developed Aug 27, 1955. Detroit, Mich.
Taken in the back yard of our home at 11093 Nashville.

Developed Aug 27, 1955. Detroit, Mich.
Taken in the back yard of our home at 11093 Nashville.

Another option for the same photograph for a new save (JPEG – photo) shows below. This is now a NEW photograph with a new name (label) and will print as shown or I can crop to either the photograph or the back description for printing or sending by email. Everything previously saved is still there not changed. As with any JPEG it can be printed as the original size or the size can be adjusted up or down. The advantage with what is shown below is that it documents the full photo along with when it was scanned and by whom. Again, below is now ONE photo.

Developed Aug 27, 1955. Detroit, Mich.
Taken in the back yard of our home at 11093 Nashville.

THIS IS A
KODACOLOR PRINT
MADE BY
EASTMAN KODAK COMPANY
T. M. REGIS. U. S. PAT. OFF.
Week Ending Aug. 27, 1955
I   R   3

Front & back scanned by
xxxxxx 2001 Jan

*

Example #2

Not the clearest photograph, this was taken in 1954. This is a crop from a small snapshot photo placed on a Word Document and then words were added. A snap view was done and saved as a JPEG, then inserted here. Names were not added for this book view. All wording shown below the photo are part of the JPEG. The original full photo was of course scanned and saved with full wording also, that being done with the scan program adding extra space to the scan for words to be added in. This is currently set to print at 3" x 3.09".

1954 Wedding Day

The wedding of Pete XXXX and Mary Elizabeth XXXX
Background: LeRoy XXXX and wife, Anne XXXX
Detroit, Michigan
Scanned July 2015 by XXX XXXX

*

Example #3

The below is actually only one save as one JPEG. Each can be printed separately with or without the words. Both views are from the same day. The original 'save' is 8" high. These two photos were placed on the scanner leaving space between them. After saved, words were added.

1954 / 1955. L to R: Harry Clarence FELIX, aka ST. FELIX and son,
LeRoy Charles ST. FELIX.
Is that fish on the grill or corn? It has to be fish, per a
park setting and grandpa being the great fisherman.
It must have been a fishing trip, probably just a day.
Per the words on the grill, this is Wayne County, which would be the
Detroit area. That means grandpa & Olga came north from Toledo to visit.

Olga (KUNTZ) FELIX, aka ST. FELIX
and step granddaughter, Gail Christine ST. FELIX.

It looks like Gail had been swimming.
These two photos appear to be 1954 or 1955.
The two photos were taken on the same day.

It appears the photos were taken by Anne C (FLINT) ST. FELIX.
Photos scanned by Donna M. ST. FELIX 2009 July.

*

Example #4

This snapshot was taken about 1921. The original and two enlarged crops were done and saved. All was placed on a Word Document and then the words were typed out. A snap view was taken and saved as a JPEG (a fourth view). That JPEG showing all three views is placed here in a size to fit this page. The top or the bottom can each be printed with or without wording. These were scanned in color (sepia tone). Printing of any save (the original, the crops or this new JPEG) can be done in color or black & white.

Ca 1921 Dayton, Ohio or Detroit, Michigan

Edward G. Seaman and new step-son, LeRoy C. XXXXXX.

*

54

Example #5

The following example also shows in my other book but I am adding it here as it is a novelty with what you can find concerning photographs.

This 1936 photo is one of those old dime store, photo booth, machine prints that come on a strip, each photo being about 1"or so tall. This was one torn off of the strip by the person in the photo and sent to her brother, his daughter many years later sending it to me.

The light marred areas in the small photo turned out to be finger prints, that done by touching it before it was dry.

One original scan that was done was sized large for detail cropping. Without size adjustment it is 9" tall if printed without resizing for printing. Resizing that, with new save names (labels), is shown here in two sizes.

Although the original photo is black & white, this was scanned in color and black & white. The color print brings out the fingerprints.

Anne Christine FLINT
Age 16. 1936
A dime store machine photo cut from the strip and sent to brother, Bill FLINT.
- Enlargement -
Two beige areas are her fingerprints as taken from machine wet.

You can see the entire photo including the edges as it was cropped to show it in full. The scan background is the lighter edging. The enlargement brings out the finger prints.

*

Example #6

This is being shown with most information removed as it tells a long family story, part being why there are two photographs alike with the center one being trimmed.

The point with showing this is that you can turn multi photos into one JPEG and put a very long story with it. With this full story, this prints out at 11" high without resizing for printing. For placement here, a crop was done to crop out words and then it was saved with a new label so the original with the full story is not changed. This is the cropped version.

1950, a guess of December. Winter 1950.

*

Example #7

This shows the original small photo, the photo back and an enlarged crop that was done of the newly married couple. The entire view below is one JPEG entered here. This can be cropped to print the top or bottom view by itself, with or without the words.

ca 1921 Newly Married

Harry C. XXXX and wife, Olga XXXXX

Now living in Toledo, Ohio

*

60

Example #8

This example shows a 1953 Kodacolor Print. The original is on top, an enlargement cropped is at the bottom. The middle view is saved as a black and white view. The Kodacolor Print information is from the back of the original. These four items and description are saved as one JPEG.

1953 Christmas Holiday Season

At the home of Anne's sister, Marie XXXX.
LeRoy XXXX with Carey, Donna with Dianne, Gail with Susie, Anne XXXX

Scanned by Donna XXXX Aug 1999

Example #9

This view shows you some of what NOT to do.

1. The top of the photograph edge was not scanned.

2. There should be only the year and maybe the place on the bottom boarder of the original photo, if anything at all.

3. The first line of information should be the largest text. That first line should read 1952 Niagara Falls.

4. The area with names should be smaller than the first intro line.

5. The information about the day and people should be written better and without any questions in it.

This appears to be 1952 and Carey is 'in the oven'.
Niagra Falls.
Carey, Mom: Anne (FLINT) ST. FELIX, grandma: Mary Elizabeth (QUINN) ST. FELIX - SEAMAN (prior to her marriage to Pete Lehnert), and Donna.

Note the same print dresses our mom made for us.
Can you imagine dressing in heels and a dress today and dressing kids up to go tramping around Niagra Falls? The way of the time! You didn't go out unless you were 'dressed up and presentable'.

Photo taken by LeRoy C. ST. FELIX, son to Mary.
Scanned by Donna M. ST. FELIX 2009 July.

*

64

Example #10

This shows the back of an old photograph where there is some explanation on the lower back added to the old documentation shown on the back.

The back shows where the photo was taken (red ink on the original), who the person is and their age. Someone else in pencil lightly wrote the year as 1952.

The explanation added below the view, on a new JPEG, is to explain who wrote the person's name and age and who wrote the year of 1952. It was two people, the mother and the paternal grandfather or grandmother. This is a photo that came back home years after being given away.

Gail at 2 yrs.' by mom, Anne. Large '1952' by Grandpa FELIX, aka ST. FELIX or his wife, Olga.

*

Example #11

This is two original photos scanned and then those were used to make a new photo (one JPEG photo). Both are the original size and as you can see they are on the same day but are different sizes. The larger one also has a little smaller boarder on it. This tells me that the larger one is one of extras that were made.

The way they show together appears visually odd and a decision has to be made to size them the same or if to use them separately.

The space to add words goes down to just above the dotted line shown below the view.

....

With those two views shown as one, the final decision was made to leave the two as shown and do an explanation as to why there are two sizes and details about the day. The two were also redone separately with information and a third view, shown below, was made using the smaller view.

In total there are nine JPEGS (photos) now saved in the folder for those two photographs. As previously mentioned, those with blank areas or words can be cropped to the photo for printing only the photograph, if wanted.

The one folder contents are:

1:    The two original fronts with space to add information (blank information).

2: The two original backs.

3: The two original fronts with information added.

4:   The two showing in one view as previously shown with no information added.

5. The same as #4 but with information added.

6:   The smaller photo with excess space removed and set into a frame, shown below.

Example #12

The following, a passport photo, was put together for a family gathering to be printed and passed out. Everyone was also given a CD containing the full passport pages and a JPEG (photo) as shown below on it so they could share with others. The below was made to print on 8 1/2" x 11" photo paper. It shows the photo and states the size of it from the family 1921 passport, an extra photo taken but not used, the names, years of birth of each and a short summary about the husband and first child arriving in the USA earlier, plus a few condensed other details.

...

Anyone who received this on CD can choose to print it as is or they can crop to any area and print it separately and at the size they choose to print it out as. As shown here it is one photo (jpeg).

If it is printed as is, even as a crop, it will print at the size it was when placed on the CD. If someone wants to print the top photo at the original size, the measurement is shown in the text so they can adjust the size.

If someone wants to make a mural, they can enlarge to the size they are happy with and do that too. The only thing that can stop major enlargements is the quality of the photograph when it was first taken and the quality of the original scan that was done of it.

PASSPORT PHOTO 1921
Geesina (ZWEEP) FLINT and the Six Youngest Children of Seven

Original used on the passport the size is 2 15/16" x 1 12" tall.
Arrival at Ellis Island on Sept 7, 1920 on the S.S. New Amsterdam. Sponsor was husband, A. F. FLINT.

Ben, Geezina, Anne, Bill, Frank, John, Marie
Dutch names:
Bernard Cornelis (1914), Geezina (1876), Geesina Annachina (1920),
Willem Frederick (1909), Augustinus Franciscus (1912), Jan Marinus (1905), Maria Elizabeth (1916)
The passport is in the custody of Nick FLINT, son to Ben.

An extra photo taken and not used.
Bill, Geezina, John, Frank, Anne, Marie, Ben
This is a remake from the original. It is unknown who has the original.

Arriving earlier was husband, Augustinus Franciscus FLINT (age 37) and their first son, Jake (age 17).
Husband Augustinus departed for the USA between January 6 -15, 1920 and saw his youngest daughter,
Anne, for the first in Sept when the balance of the family arrived in the USA.

Scanned by Donna M. ST. FELIX, 2001

Example #13

This example is a photograph scan that was sent to me. It is not clear or straight but it is the only one I have to work with so this is an example of making do with what you have.

The very tiny view I received was enlarged, copied to a Word Document, some history was added, a snap crop was done and that was saved as a JPEG, shown below.

Squiar Asbury BOND

Born 1815, Ohio. Buried Morrison Hill, Illinois
Married #1 Susan MACKEY 23 Feb 1840 Preble Co. Ohio.
Eight children.
Married #2 Sarah Catherine TAYLOR 2 Apr 1872, Republic Co., Kansas.
One of their sons, John Ward BOND, born 15 Apr 1877, Bellvue, Kansas
had a son William who married Mable L. HUNDLE 9 Apr 1902.
With Mable he had two children, one being Ward Edwin BOND,
born 9 Apr 1903 Benkelman, Nebraska. Died 5 Nov 1960, Dallas, Texas.
Ward was a well-known actor in Hollywood.

*

Example #14

Above is a view of the back of an early professional photograph. This shows who took the photograph long with the address, city and the state of where the photo was taken at. Tracking the photographer at that address gave me the possible years that the photograph was taken.

The corners are true to the original photograph as it was scanned 'over' the edges.

Chapter Eleven. Main Steps in Summary

1: Take &/or make good notes for each photograph and organize them.

2: Sort your photos using envelopes.

3: Start making your computer files for storing scans and notes.

4: Scan your photos x 100%, also doing enlargements and enlarged crops. Take your time naming them. Remember to give each new scan a new label by changing or adding at least one letter, word or number.

6: Place scans in the correct folder.

7: Go back thru each folder after scanning is done or after each photo is scanned, to add organized, condensed information to your choice of photos into the blank area scanned below the photograph. Save with a new label. (Add 'w words' or 'words' to the label so as not to alter the original scan.)

8. Return any borrowed photographs. If they are your own, store the originals in archive materials in a dry, dark area. LABEL the box/s. It helps for organization to make a note on the box, and add a note into the box, saying that the items have been scanned.

Do some practicing with photos that have no sentimental meaning to you to avoid excess light on older photographs.

FREE programs used in various steps described in this book:

A free word document program:
http://www.openoffice.org/download/index.html

Photo Adjustments: www.FastStone.org

Screen Shots - MWSnap: www.mirekw.com

Frames on line: http://www.fotor.com

The author has no connection to any site or program mentioned in this book other than the free unsolicited use of the program.

78

A note from the author.

If this book did help you or give you new ideas, your favorable feedback to where you purchased the book is very much appreciated.

Current books by KALTEN
and news on upcoming books can be found at

http://BooksByKalten.blogspot.com

www.ingramcontent.com/pod-product-compliance
Lightning Source LLC
Chambersburg PA
CBHW071223280526
45787CB00002B/787